CANCER

HOROSCOPE

& ASTROLOGY

2022

Published by Mystic Cat Press

Suite SM-2380-6403

14601 North Bybee Lake Court

Portland, Oregon 97203

Phone: +1 (805) 308-6503

SiaSands@Yahoo.com

Contents

CANCER 2022
HOROSCOPE & ASTROLOGY

Four Weeks Per Month

Week 1 – Days 1 - 7

Week 2 – Days 8 - 14

Week 3 – Days 15 - 21

Week 4 – Days 22 – Month-end

CANCER

Cancer Dates: June 21st to July 22nd
Symbol: Crab
Element: Water
Planet: Moon
House: Fourth
Colors: Silver, white

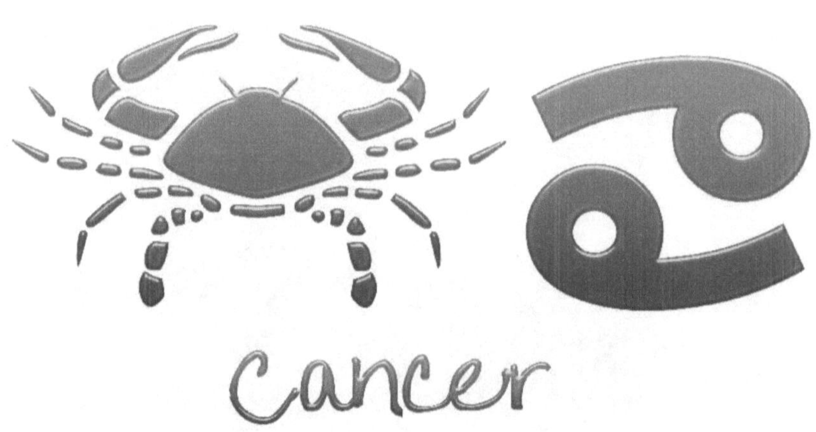

2022 AT A GLANCE

Eclipses

Partial Solar – April 30th

Total Lunar – May 16th

Partial Solar – October 25th

Total Lunar -November 8th

Equinoxes and Solstices

Spring - March 20th

Summer - June 21st

Fall – September 23rd

Winter – December 21st

Mercury Retrogrades

January 14th, Aquarius - February 4th Capricorn

May 10th, Gemini - June 3rd, Taurus

September 10th, Libra - October 2nd Virgo

December 29th, Capricorn - January 1st, 2023, Capricorn

2022 FULL MOONS

Wolf Moon: January 17th, 23:48.

Snow Moon: February 16th, 16:57

Worm Moon March 18th, 07:17

Pink Moon: April 16th, 18:54

Flower Moon: May 16th, 04:13

Strawberry Moon: June 14th, 11:51

Buck Moon: July 13th, 18:37

Sturgeon Moon: August 12th, 01:35

Corn, Harvest Moon: September 10th, 09:59

Hunters Moon: October 9th, 20:54

Beaver Moon: November 8th, 11:01

Cold Moon: December 8th, 04:07

THE MOON PHASES

New Moon (Dark Moon)

Waxing Crescent Moon

First Quarter Moon

Waxing Gibbous Moon

Full Moon

Waning Gibbous (Disseminating) Moon

Third (Last/Reconciling) Quarter Moon

Waning Crescent (Balsamic) Moon

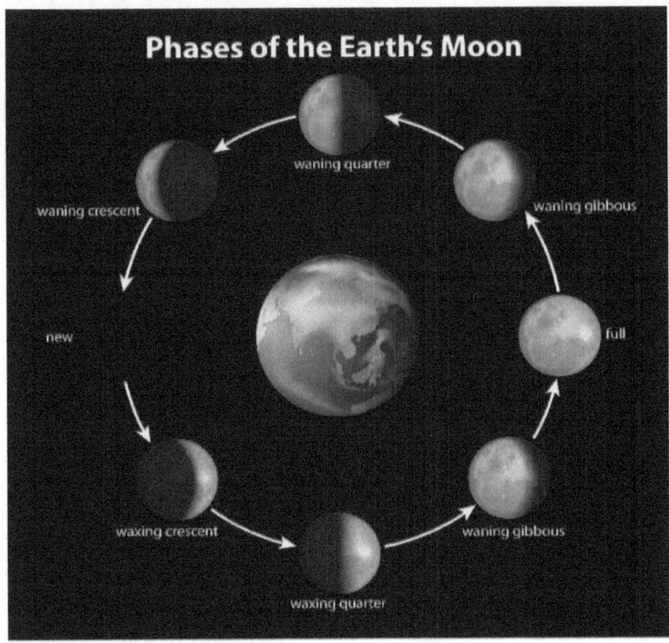

2022

JANUARY

M	T	W	T	F	S	S
					1	2
3	4	5	6	7	8	9
10	11	12	13	14	15	16
17	18	19	20	21	22	23
24	25	26	27	28	29	30
31						

FEBRUARY

M	T	W	T	F	S	S
	1	2	3	4	5	6
9	10	11	12	11	12	13
14	15	16	17	18	19	20
21	22	23	24	25	26	27
28						

MARCH

M	T	W	T	F	S	S
	1	2	3	4	4	6
7	8	9	10	11	12	13
14	15	16	17	18	19	20
21	22	23	24	25	26	27
28	29	30	31			

APRIL

M	T	W	T	F	S	S
				1	2	3
4	5	6	7	8	9	10
11	12	13	14	15	16	17
18	19	20	21	22	23	24
25	26	27	28	29	30	

MAY

M	T	W	T	F	S	S
						1
2	3	4	5	6	7	8
9	10	11	12	13	14	15
16	17	18	19	20	21	22
23	24	25	26	27	28	29
30	31					

JUNE

M	T	W	T	F	S	S
		1	2	3	4	5
6	7	8	9	10	11	12
13	14	15	16	17	18	19
20	21	22	23	24	25	26
27	28	29	30			

JULY

M	T	W	T	F	S	S
				1	2	3
4	5	6	7	8	9	10
11	12	13	14	15	16	17
18	19	20	21	22	23	24
25	26	27	28	29	30	31

AUGUST

M	T	W	T	F	S	S
1	2	3	4	5	6	7
8	9	10	11	12	13	14
15	16	17	18	19	20	21
22	23	24	25	26	27	28
29	30	31				

SEPTEMBER

M	T	W	T	F	S	S
			1	2	3	4
5	6	7	8	9	10	11
12	13	14	15	16	17	18
19	20	21	22	23	24	25
26	27	28	29	30		

OCTOBER

M	T	W	T	F	S	S
					1	2
3	4	5	6	7	8	9
10	11	12	13	14	15	16
17	18	19	20	21	22	23
24	25	26	27	28	29	30
31						

NOVEMBER

M	T	W	T	F	S	S
	1	2	3	4	5	6
7	8	9	10	11	12	13
14	15	16	17	18	19	20
21	22	23	24	25	26	27
28	29	30				

DECEMBER

M	T	W	T	F	S	S
			1	2	3	4
5	6	7	8	9	10	11
12	13	14	15	16	17	18
19	20	21	22	23	24	25
26	27	28	29	30	31	

Time set to Coordinated Universal Time Zone

(UT±0)

Meteor Showers are on the date they peak.

JANUARY

Sun	Mon	Tue	Wed	Thu	Fri	Sat
						1
2	3	4	5	6	7	8
9	10	11	12	13	14	15
16	17	18	19	20	21	22
23	24	25	26	27	28	29
30	31					

January 2nd - New Moon in Capricorn 18:33

January 3rd - Quadrantids Meteor Shower. January 1st-5th.

January 7th - Mercury at Greatest Eastern Elongation

January 9th - First Quarter Moon in Aries 18:11

January 14th - Mercury Retrograde begins in Aquarius

January 17th - Wolf Moon. Full Moon in Cancer 23:48

January 25th - Last Quarter Moon Scorpio 13:42

NEW MOON

The Quadrantids Meteor Shower brings a changing landscape that lights up expansion. It reboots and renews your energy on many levels. It is an excellent time to release energetic blocks and focus on building your social life. There is more stability on offer. It brings opportunities to socialize and mingle that nurture harmony and well-being. It's a freedom-driven environment that lets you dive into engaging experiences as you embrace the options that support expansion in your social life. It brings a time of exploring the possibilities that kick off a lovely phase of personal growth. It lets you avoid drama by shedding outworn skins and removing people who limit your energy. It brings a huge turning point as new friendships emerge that inspire your spirit. It is a vibrant landscape that takes shape ahead.

Things are on the move this week as you enter a productive time of progressing your goals. An original path arrives that sees you chasing a lead and investigating your options. It brings a happy and active environment with less stress or worries. It helps you take care of business and simplify your life. It grounds your foundations as it stabilizes your home environment. It marks the beginning of a robust phase that is a ticket to growing your circumstances. You achieve maximum results by ferreting out unique options. Planning and strategizing form the basis of this enterprising week.

Mercury Retrograde begins in Aquarius at the week's end. As you overcome challenges during the entire Mercury Retrograde phase, you navigate an uncertain environment and discover pathways that take you towards growth. It brings an extended time that offers rejuvenation, reinvention, and ultimately, transformation. It advances your skills to a new level and does see you delving into areas that grow your abilities. New adventures come calling, and this lets you broaden your reach and branch out into enterprising areas. Magic and creativity allow you to forge an innovative path towards your vision. It helps you brew up an exciting landscape of possibility.

Being prudent and selective is wise. It helps you weed out the drama lamas and distance yourself from areas that limit progress. You soon discover a new chapter that breathes life into your surroundings. Widening your abilities grows an avenue that nurtures your skills. It paves the way for peace and balance to blossom in your world. You release areas that dampen your spirit and cling to your energy. It sets in motion a time of setting goals and achieving gold. It plays an essential part that becomes therapeutic and beneficial to you on a soul level. It does show a journey that develops your skills and share your passion with a broader audience. It offers an avenue that lets you give back to others and nurture community spirit. You are gifted with a strong sense of compassion and empathy and have a splendid ability that fosters harmony.

The Wolf Moon. Full Moon in Cancer this week is a new chapter on many levels. You explore side avenues of growth. Curious changes ahead bring improvement. You get a better sense of clarity about the direction along. It does bring an upgrade; a favorable event places you in the right alignment to connect with a project that inspires your mind. It has you in sync with others who bring a valuable sense of support and connection. Everything is grounded and stable as you start expanding your social life. Taking the initiative draws dividends. It marks a significant turning point. You begin to see your vision taking shape. It rules a time of expansion and increasing harmony. It rebalances your energy and draws stability into your foundations. It transitions to a more social time that tempts you to connect with friends. It creates foundations that offer room to grow and prosper. The path ahead glimmers with new possibilities. Productivity and expansion are the basis from which to expand your world.

You discover an area that offers consistency, progression, and balance. It lets you spread your wings, and as your dreams take flight, you enjoy smoother sailing. It brings a shift forward that flexes your abilities into a new area. It helps you direct your restless energy correctly by creating space for developing projects that inspire and motivate. It sets the stage for a journey where you can achieve growth.

You dive into an abundant landscape that offers expansion. It lets you establish a stable foundation from which to engage in connecting with your tribe. A whirlwind of activity brings new options to contemplate. You tune into a broader picture of what is possible and get involved with developing your skills.

A passageway opens that offers a course of learning and advancement. Going after your dreams brings good fortune; it marks a significant time that elevates your role. It brings something on offer that smacks of groundbreaking potential; it lets you create a change you have been seeking. Opportunity comes knocking. A path of adventure transitions you forward towards a journey you can grow.

Advancing your situation is a top priority; it kicks off an exciting chapter that merges with your social life. It brings expansion, and this guides you towards a path that glitters with new possibilities. It paints a landscape that is social and connected as you mingle with friends. You touch down on a chapter that inspires and rejuvenates your life soon. It brings change and growth; it lets you drift away from areas no longer relevant while encouraging you to investigate new leads. Shifting your perspective to an abundant mindset draws dividends. It takes you forward towards a specific time of improved stability. It is an enriching chapter that illustrates the blessings in your world.

FEBRUARY

Sun	Mon	Tue	Wed	Thu	Fri	Sat
		1	2	3	4	5
6	7	8	9	10	11	12
13	14	15	16	17	18	19
20	21	22	23	24	25	26
27	28					

February 1st - New Moon in Aquarius 05:45
February 1st - Chinese New Year (Tiger)
February 1st - Imbolc

February 4th - Mercury Retrograde ends in Capricorn

February 8th - First Quarter Moon in Taurus 13:50

February 16th - Mercury at Greatest Western Elongation
February 16th - Snow Moon. Full Moon in Leo 16:57

February 23rd - Last Quarter Moon in Scorpio 22:32

NEW MOON

Things are on the move for your social life; it helps you sweep away what no longer serves your highest good. It brings a journey of growing your world and sharing experiences and thoughts with a broader range of friends. It brings a social environment into focus, and lively conversations draw renewal and rejuvenation. The good news arrives that sparks excitement as it offers expansion and growth. The thing is, new possibilities are coming into your world soon; it brings a change of scene that draws emerging abundance. It brings a more social environment that heightens confidence. It does bring changes to your social life.

You hone in on a new chapter and receive wind of potential that inspires and motivates change. It lets you lift the lid on a new journey that beckons you forward. Looking at your long-term goals is helpful, as it enables you to adjust the course as necessary. An intriguing opportunity comes knocking and invites you to discover the full potential possible. Being proactive lets, you uncover a lead worth growing.

It may be useful to expand your horizons into new areas. Reshuffling the decks of fate draws a pursuit that sparks your interest. It correlates with plenty of new energy coming into your world to lighten the load and sweep you off on a new adventure. Exploring the options available helps open a path that offers room to progress.

There is an improvement coming around home life. Opportunities ahead link up to a more social environment. A changing scene on the horizon leaves you feeling optimistic about the future. It brings the building of stable foundations that gently progress things forward. It lights up activity in the areas of creativity and social life. News arrives that helps you take steps towards outlining your plan for future growth. Setting your aspirations is vital.

Getting to know someone better draws dividends. It offers support and lets you expand your social circle. It brings improvement to your home life. You discover this person is wise and possesses an openness that is enriching and abundant. Focusing on developing a friendship gives you a glimpse of what is possible with this companion. It lights up a journey of valuable insights that provides clarity into the direction ahead.

It brings a time of surprises and spontaneity that offers a chance to mingle and network with others. It has you thinking about the future in a different light. It does bring a social environment that draws abundance and joy. Lively discussions bring solutions, and thoughtful gestures bring a surge of well-being that hit a sweet note for your social life. It is a happy time that lets you fan the fires of your inspiration with an active and productive journey forward.

The Full Moon in Leo this week does wipe the slate clean on many levels. Personal sacrifice has been too prominent in your past life. Now you have an opportunity to nurture your home environment. An emphasis on reaching for your dreams grounds your energy in a productive environment. You exact positive change by being open to new pathways. It rekindles your creativity and guides you to a path that glitters with possibility. Reshuffling the decks of potential brings new possibilities to lighten your mood. It brings the opportunity to heal the broken parts and nourish your soul. It holds a journey of security and abundance.

Use this Full Moon's power to focus on what you can do and don't worry about limitations. Life is a changing parade, and flexibility allows you to evolve. The next chapter is a beauty; abundance loves the void, you grow and prosper through the challenges you overcome. Something ahead that brings a boost. You've known your fair share of troubles, which has got you plenty of resilience and grit. As things begin to settle down, you can realign aspects of life that feel frayed or disruptive. It lets you move forward without strain or worry. Grounding your energy creates space to nurture creativity and inspiration. It reboots your potential and brings blessings you can appreciate. New options crop up to inspire change and growth.

Your career path ahead is heading to an upswing. An expansive arena comes into view; it's a time dreaming fresh possibilities that guide progress. It does see you moving away from areas that limit and restrict your potential. It brings a busy time that lets you move up the ladder towards success. It gives you a chance to sharpen your skills and gain a wealth of experience. Concentrating on your vision enables you to dial down stress and embrace inspiration.

New projects and endeavors bring a lighter atmosphere. It improves security around your home life and does offer the kind of advancement that you can grow. You embark on a meaningful chapter of growth and development. Sudden bursts of creativity draw brainstorming sessions that kick-off effective planning. It marks a bold beginning that brings joy and inspiration. An abundant mindset broadens the playing field.

A happy chapter is coming; it lets you embrace social activities and a sense of connection. You may be feeling drawn to artistic expression and find an endeavor that absorbs your restless energy. It brings a creative element and does offer social benefits as well. Connecting with a broader community environment draws a sense of support that nurtures well-being. It lets you leave behind old wounds as you enjoy a fresh, emotional start.

MARCH

Sun	Mon	Tue	Wed	Thu	Fri	Sat
		1	2	3	4	5
6	7	8	9	10	11	12
13	14	15	16	17	18	19
20	21	22	23	24	25	26
27	28	29	30	31		

March 2nd - New Moon in Pisces 17:34

March 10th - First Quarter Moon in Gemini 10:45

March 18th - Worm Moon. Full Moon in Virgo 07:17

March 20th - Ostara/Spring Equinox 15:33

March 25th - Last Quarter Moon in Capricorn 05:37

FULL MOON

New Moon in Pisces reveals a new undercurrent of potential that surrounds your life. The news is coming that reshapes goals and lets you plot a course to a new growth level. It draws a bustling phase of activity that is enterprising and productive. Investing wisely in developing this area lets you take advantage of new inspiration and options that heighten creativity. Life becomes balanced as security improves. Laying the groundwork one step at a time develops this option beautifully.

Life takes a curious turn when new information is unlocked. It does set a mission in place, and you head off on a new adventure. It brings a clear incentive to ramp up motivation and progress forward. An active time of growth gives you the fuel necessary to increase your reach and dabble in an area that inspires your interest. If you have felt restricted recently, that lifts as you tap into this abundant stream of potential.

You lighten the load when an offer crosses your path that offers a bounty of potential. If you have struggled with the changes swirling you around your life, you reveal a new area that provides joy and growth. It provides a beneficial option that lets you tap into underutilized talents. It brings creative options to light that give you an empowering sense of having solutions at your disposal.

You reveal an enterprising option that gets the ball rolling on developing the path ahead. You can shake off the doldrums and connect with a broader world of potential. You discover a piece of fascinating information that provides insight into an interpersonal bond. Focusing on deepening a situation that captures your inspiration does create a happy shift forward. It's a compliment to your lifestyle; it gives you the motivation to navigate complex environments and keep working towards your vision.

It shines a light on a productive chapter. It creates the basis from which you can expand your social life. Deepening friendships stimulate your mind and encourage an expansive outlook. It does have you feeling lighter and ready to step out in a more connected environment with enthusiasm. It's tailor-made for cooking up dreamy plans and sharing experiences with another person.

Your creative abilities are sharp in manifestation. You can spot the potential in a diverse opportunity that comes your way soon. Expanding your life draws happiness, luck, and growth. An area you become involved with is the ticket for improving your circumstances. It brings a memorable phase that offers change, discovery, and adventure to good effect. A sense of buoyancy carries you forward to new experiences.

A Full Moon in Virgo this week. At the end of the week, Ostara/Spring Equinox brings the Sun again after the long winter. It brings forward movement that expands your options. It begins a trend that lets you grow your world, and this brings the type of potential that offers self-development and growth. Practical advice from a knowledgeable person proves to be invaluable. It clears the deck to explore a direction that develops your abilities. It sees you taking on a new assignment that showcases your skills.

It lets you take advantage of new potential; it brings news of a progression that draws an influx of business. Focusing on the most important goals and priorities enables you to streamline responsibilities and continue to develop this area. Progress is dynamic and fluid, allowing you to navigate hurdles and sidestep issues. Innovative thinking and a creative approach are handy tools that help you make the most of this time.

It brings a more prosperous life experience and sets a positive trend. The warmth of friendship and support of others nurtures your spirit. Exciting developments shine a light on passion and adventure. You get immersed in an area that shows depth and range; it lets you reach something more. Your ability to withstand the storm, and navigate complex environments, takes you towards developing hopes and dreams.

Life becomes a whirlwind, and it does bring new options to contemplate. An experimental flavor puts a unique flair on the possibilities ahead. It renews energy and helps you embark on a phase of expansion. A new beginning brings the inspiration necessary to push back barriers and delve into new areas. Helpful ideas and suggestions help build strong foundations around your home life. A surprise arrives, and it brings a boost of lighter energy.

There is some restructuring ahead that can leave you feeling uncertain. A breakthrough arrives that draws new responsibilities. It does see something new on offer that takes your talents to a higher level. It adds more pressure, but the rewards offer greater security. It does launch your abilities forward.

Advancing your career brings a busy time that is active and productive. Life takes a fortunate turn when news arrives that brings blessings. It lights up pathways of creativity and imagination. It offers a direct link towards an enterprising time. Being in the prime position to develop your goals creates growth. It brings progress to a project that lights a path forward that offers an outstanding opportunity to refine and develop your talents. Taking time to plan the course methodically sees you reaching for an endeavor that elevates your abilities. News arrives that brings an exciting option into focus.

APRIL

Sun	Mon	Tue	Wed	Thu	Fri	Sat
					1	2
3	4	5	6	7	8	9
10	11	12	13	14	15	16
17	18	19	20	21	22	23
24	25	26	27	28	29	30

April 1st - New Moon in Aries 06:24

April 9th - First Quarter Moon in Cancer 06:47

April 16th - Pink Moon. Full Moon in Libra 18:54

April 22nd - Lyrids Meteor Shower from April 16-25

April 23rd - Last Quarter Moon in Aquarius 11:56.

April 29th - Mercury Greatest Eastern Elongation of 20.6 degrees from the Sun.

April 30th - New Moon in Taurus 20:27

New Moon in Aries this week gives the green light to move forward towards developing an area of interest. Specific goals you have in mind reach fruition, and this lets your imagination blossom. It brings exciting changes that draw lightness into your world. You get the chance to grow your talents and evolve your path to a new level. It speaks about expansive horizons, something curious is in the pipeline that cracks the code to developing harmony and wellness. You make smart choices, and this brings a breakthrough.

Research ahead immerses you in developing a dream project. Your visionary ideas offer a passageway towards growth. Information arrives that lights the path forward, allowing you to build a tangible trajectory that provides results. As your situation flows along, you move towards developing an endeavor that grows your abilities. Staying true to your original ideas brings a turning point.

The troubles and complexities you faced have taught you the value of resilience. It has given you the wisdom needed to navigate tricky environments and come out with a winner. You set sail on a timely voyage that expands your world. It draws new options to light. Life comes full circle soon, and this connects you with someone from a previous chapter. It is an aspiring trend that expands your social life with new and old contacts coming forward.

The path ahead clears as you reveal a fantastic landscape of new possibilities. It gives you a chance to rebrand your image and reinvent yourself in a new area. Understanding the broader picture's relevance cracks the code to nurturing a meaningful and well-designed journey that supports well-being. You get involved with a trip that offers self-development and growth; it draws blessings into your life.

There are changes ahead for your career path. It gets you involved with learning a new area, and you take on a course that inspires growth. It heightens productivity and has you working efficiently and effectively to grow your working environment. Developing your goals brings a focus on advancement. It lets you harness leadership abilities and expand your reach into a journey worth growing. Soon, it takes you towards a faster-moving and more active environment. You are on the road to improving your career prospects.

A conversation ahead ignites a social phase. It lights up the area of developing a friendship as it involves more social and community options. A golden exchange with another nurtures well-being and brings a boost to your life. It helps you on many levels as it improves optimism and brings the motivation to expand your horizons. It does see you reaching for a brighter and more stable landscape. As you form a more robust network of support, it draws abundance into your world. It brings a time of sharing ideas and growing your social life.

There is incoming potential likely to surge as you enter an extended time that brings change and rewards your situation with new options. As you navigate forward, you get a strong sense of heightened security, lifting you towards advancement. It is a busy and vibrant time that motivates and invigorates your spirit. Ambitions and aspirations are aided by a flow of manifestation, bringing sunny skies overhead. Something on offer catches your eye.

Creating space to nurture your social life draws dividends. It does bring a shift forward that opens the path. It takes you towards a person who catches your eye. An impromptu meeting gets a chance to talk openly; a closer bond takes shape. It does shine a light on building a foundation that is stable and secure. You are on the same page as this person as they seek a similar destination. This person has a good sense of humor and an optimistic outlook.

Events lineup beautifully to nourish your life. It does bring an engaging chapter of sharing thoughts and ideas with others on the same wavelength. You have enormous potential to improve your home life and advance your goals towards their destination. It places your talents in the spotlight, and there is a strong focus on developing an area that captures your interest. News arrives by surprise that hits a sweet note for your social life.

Lyrids Meteor Shower brings a powerhouse of fresh energy into your environment. It does get communication out of the left field that arrives by surprise. You touch down on sharing thoughts and memories with someone who has been out of the loop lately. Connecting with this person draws well-being. It does bring valuable advice and guidance that help give you a better idea of the direction ahead. It enables you to broaden your horizon and become more confident about developing your world.

This week brings opportunities to socialize. Your willingness to stay open to new experiences and people brings luck and good fortune into your world. It drives a phase of wanderlust, as opportunities ahead get expansion in your social life. The more you push back the boundaries in your world, the more you encourage the right landscape to blossom. A sunny aspect ahead flings open new potential.

Soon enough, you see positive signs that feel encouraging. It puts a focus on freedom and expansion. It increases your enthusiasm for life as lighter energy flows into your surroundings. Life becomes busier; it does bring a bond closer. You are ready to open a new book chapter. This person values your friendship and support.

MAY

Sun	Mon	Tue	Wed	Thu	Fri	Sat
1	2	3	4	5	6	7
8	9	10	11	12	13	14
15	16	17	18	19	20	21
22	23	24	25	26	27	28
29	30	31				

May 6th - Eta Aquarids Meteor Shower, April 19th - May 28th

May 9th - First Quarter Moon in Leo 00:21

May 10th - Mercury Retrograde begins in Gemini

May 16th - Total Lunar Eclipse 01:32

May 16th - Flower Moon. Full Moon in Scorpio 04:13

May 22nd - Last Quarter Moon in Aquarius 18:43

May - 30th - New Moon in Leo 00:21

FULL MOON

Eta Aquarids Meteor Shower brings a time of expansion, freedom, and optimism. You have gifts to share with a broader audience, and getting involved with developing your talents unearths latent abilities. Something is on offer soon that hits the right note. Your willingness to help others is admirable. There is an option to assist another soon; being of service brings opportunities into your world that enrich your life. A bounty of fresh options tempts growth and expansion.

Removing limiting energy allows you to let go of stress and release old emotions. The outworn scatter to the wind, and this is so liberating. It ushers in new energy, healing, and grace. You have a unique ability to draw well-being and harmony into your world. Exploring ways to improve your circumstances brings a journey worth growing. It provides you with broader options that tempt you forward.

Feeling secure helps you turn a corner and head towards growth. The changes and adjustments you make draw smoother sailing. A new chapter of potential is currently emerging, and there is an emphasis on growing your abilities. A fresh wind of possibility brings new options to contemplate. It draws balance and harmony and does help you build foundations that offer security. Your intuition is rising, letting you become more perceptive and sensitive to vibrations that guide the path ahead. It ratchets up what is possible and soon sees you diving into a dream role.

Mercury retrograde causes mayhem and disruption in your social life when it begins in Gemini this week. There may be a lack of closure around a situation that caused issues for you. A necessary transition is occurring, and this releases the outworn energy. It clears the slate and draws acceptance around a problem where there may have been some regrets—optimism soon blossoms in the wake of this healing. As you release outworn energy, you create space for the new potential to flow into your world. It releases stress and beautifully aligns you with a shift forward. It encourages expansion. Re-examining your vision, you make changes that offer a streamlined path towards your dream. Any tweaks or adjustments are about focusing on the important stuff.

Beginning a new journey brings feelings of joy and anticipation. A time of blossoming creativity is looming. You are in a time of transition as a past cycle is ending. It does bring up emotional awareness around sensitive areas. Creating space to heal and release the past is a vital part of stepping into the future potential. You create space for a path that draws new possibilities to light. It brings an enriching chapter that sees you laying the groundwork for a new journey forward. It creates the basis from which you grow your dreams.

Flower Moon. Full Moon in Scorpio signifies you are ready to close the book on hardship. Resolving outworn energy and healing the past brings a complete overhaul to overdue areas. As you remove the outworn power, you gain insight into which direction is best to develop next. Your transition to a higher level of advancement brings opportunities for self-development and growth.

You are ready to find your correct path. A transition ahead brings heightened opportunities. You find value in being generous and open with your talents and time. It takes you closer to your real purpose. It lets you nurture a path that leads to your higher self. It brings emotional abundance and gives you a chance to reinvent yourself in an area that draws meaning and plenty. It brings a slower pace as it draws rejuvenation, which lets you build stable foundations. It gives you everything you need to feel secure and grow your world.

If you feel stuck in a holding pattern, new opportunities will soon get the ball rolling on a productive chapter. Once you get an idea of the progress possible, it gives you the confidence to take in new adventures. A sense of wanderlust encourages expansion. It does bring a chance to progress your abilities and develop your talents in a new area. You discover an outlet for your restless energy, and it ramps up the fun in your world.

A New Moon in Leo brings insight. As the confusion lifts, you gain insight into the path ahead. Being mindful of your goals and dreams helps pave the way for a smoother trajectory forward. It brings momentum into your life, and you dare to expand your horizons and open a new chapter. You begin to spot clues that suggest advancement is imminent. It has you feeling fantastic about your emotional life. It brings heartwarming communication that brings happy news. It keeps your life humming along. It is a welcome distraction and draws well-being and abundance into your world. A fresh opportunity arrives that offers the chance to improve your skills. It does give a push towards advancement. It is a golden venture that captivates your attention. Research and planning offer the best results as you prepare to put your 1st foot forward on developing a journey that grows your abilities. Making inquiries, keeping your eyes open helps you spot the gemstone ahead.

Your accomplishments receive recognition; valuable feedback offers insight into your performance. It does let you make strides towards achieving a pleasing result. It sets the stage for further progression, and you soon awaken to a sense of creativity that inspires change. Moving out of your comfort zone brings an opportunity to grow in a new area. The borders of your life expand and get an exciting destination into focus. Advancement is in the pipeline; it offers a new level that captures the essence of prosperity.

JUNE

Sun	Mon	Tue	Wed	Thu	Fri	Sat
			1	2	3	4
5	6	7	8	9	10	11
12	13	14	15	16	17	18
19	20	21	22	23	24	25
26	27	28	29	30		

June 3rd - Mercury Retrograde ends in Taurus

June 7th - First Quarter Moon in Virgo 14:48

June 14th - Strawberry Moon. Full Moon in Sagittarius Supermoon 11:51

June 16th - Mercury's greatest Western elongation of 23.2 degrees from the Sun

June 21st - Last Quarter Moon in Aries 03:11

June 21st - Midsummer/Litha Solstice 09:13

June 29th - New Moon in Cancer 02:52

NEW MOON

FULL MOON

Mercury Retrograde ends in Taurus. It brings a lucky time of thinking big about future possibilities. Life becomes lighter and sweeter as you step out in a landscape of increasing chances. It lets you put your thinking cap on and dive into developing new options. Connecting with like-minded people brings a sweet note to your social life. You move to a favorable phase that lets you use your talents to a greater degree. Opportunities emerge that let you make the most of your inherent abilities. A creative venture becomes a hot topic of conversation. It does seem this endeavor is ready to shine in the spotlight. It activates a success-driven chapter of growing the potential possible.

It represents stepping into your power. It lets you find a new position, and this opportunity allows you to contribute your talents to a broader audience. Someone comes forward with guidance that helps make your dreams happen. Inspired, you lift the lid on achieving your vision. You are a force to be reckoned with, and little breaks your stride as you get involved with developing a journey that inspires growth. An experienced person teaches you the ropes and helps grow your abilities. It brings an enterprising chapter that inspires change.

The Full Moon in Sagittarius Supermoon at week's end brings a curious benefit. It is the right time to stay open to new possibilities. It gets you more involved with the path ahead; you become less of a spectator and more proactive about reaching your dreams. There will be a great many possibilities flowing into your world that tempt you towards expansion. It does bring options to work with your abilities and refine your skills. A positive trend lights the path towards an exciting destination. You may notice a build-up of restless energy; this is expected and encouraged as it gets you thinking outside of the box.

You reveal the mystery that inspires your imagination. As you explore the possibilities, sweeping changes flow into your world. It lights the path forward for developing a dream close to your heart. As personal development comes to the forefront of your life, it lets you make notable tracks on evolving your abilities to a new level. Casting your net of dreams wide opens a realm of possibilities. Information is coming that builds a robust foundation. It grounds your energy and gives you a proper direction. It shines a golden light of good fortune in your career sector. Growth and learning provide a stable basis from which to expand your world. It does let you untangle the roadblocks and red tape. It gives you the green light to work with your abilities, refine your skills, and make the most of your talents. It does see you shining in a new role soon.

Midsummer/Litha Solstice at week's end reveals an opportunity that broadens your horizons soon. Life picks up speed and becomes more active. The news arrives that brings a chance to spend time with friends. It does get a positive note that sets the stage to develop your social life. A stable foundation restores the balance and improves your home life. It is a busy time ahead that brings communication, news, and information. It lights up pathways of connection and support. It lets you build a bridge towards a lighter future. Nurturing this environment draws happiness and success.

Your willingness to explore possibilities and push back barriers plays an essential part in improving your circumstances. Staying true to your vision brings a path that offers enticing potential. It is a portal through to a happier phase that nurtures your spirit. Investing your time and energy into developing your goals brings a degree of growth. It sees inspiration returning the full force.

Exploring the potential on the periphery of your environment brings freedom and expansion. New energy is flowing around your life that lets you take steps towards a journey of growth. It pulls happiness and draws transformation. It kicks off a chapter of sunshine and sparkle, and as you continue to work with your ideas, your creativity blossoms. Your best qualities hit the spotlight, and this fuels motivation.

The New Moon in Cancer delivers an emphasis on growing your world that opens new pathways. Changes ahead provide a vital clue. You channel your restless energy into developing a journey of transformation and progression. Good news is coming as something special is on offer for you soon. It brings a fantastic direction that creates the right environment for your life to flow forward. Exploring new leads lets you come out a winner.

You soon land in a new and exciting landscape. Essential changes bring expanding opportunities. It does take you towards an active and productive environment that lets you improve your bottom line. An avenue open is that brings lighter energy. It enables you to extend your reach and create the stepping stones that take you towards success. It is instrumental in advancing your situation forward.

You can use this time to think about the path ahead. You unearth new information by doing your research. It unlocks essential information that clears the way and helps you move away from areas that limit progress. Focusing on the building blocks lets you make the vital moves that progress you toward nurturing your vision. A gateway opens that helps map out a plan for future growth.

JULY

Sun	Mon	Tue	Wed	Thu	Fri	Sat
					1	2
3	4	5	6	7	8	9
10	11	12	13	14	15	16
17	18	19	20	21	22	23
24	25	26	27	28	29	30
31						

July 7th - First Quarter Moon in Libra 02:14

July 13th - Buck Moon. Full Moon in Capricorn. Supermoon 18:37

July 20th - Last Quarter Moon in Aries 14:18

July 28th - New Moon in Leo 17:54

July 28th - Delta Aquarids Meteor Shower. July 12th - August 23rd

FULL MOON

A new option arrives, which leaves you feeling energized and excited. An attractive possibility opens the path forward. Rocketing creativity draws innovative ideas and charts a suitable course towards a new enterprise. Change is in the air as fortune aligns to form a clear window of opportunity. A cleared path is an invitation to expand horizons. It brings the time and motivation needed to develop a crucial area. It offers growth and stability; getting back to basics builds a robust foundation. A productive environment encourages harmony as it restores equilibrium.

Setting the bar higher sets a powerful intention that you deserve the best. It keeps out the riffraff and allows you to be discerning who you let into your inner circle. It does emphasize improving your life, which ultimately leads to expanded options for your social life. Your journey is evolving and moving towards greener pastures. Your willingness to unearth new possibilities brings golden moments overhead.

It speaks of releasing the stress and focusing on developing the path ahead. New information lets something special emerge in your life. The timing is ideal; it brings growth and sees a personal initiative blossom as you take the steps necessary to improve your circumstances. It brings you in contact with others who support and nurture your abilities. It offers a highly productive path that brings advancement.

The Full Moon in Capricorn is the second Supermoon for this year. Life soon settles into a more comfortable groove. It brings a reward that offers a new option. Taking a moment to pause and gain insight into the pathways that tempt you forward brings clarity. It draws an adventurous time of liberation, freedom, and expansion. It brings a time of lively discussions and the sharing of thoughts and ideas with those who support your work. Important information brings surprises news that offers a boost.

It is a pivotal time to create positive change and draw healing into your life. Removing outworn energy lights up new options. You build foundations that improved security and stability. A dream comes into focus soon, and it is one that blesses your life with new possibilities. You open a page of sharing thoughts and ideas with someone who offers advice.

It speaks of a smoother journey ahead. You are entering a phase that draws abundance. It is significant as it brings a transition to a more balanced and stable environment. It helps develop goals, and it does bring expanded awareness about areas that are worth developing. Tuning into this shift opens a new deck of potential. It brings a highly creative environment that enriches your life.

This week speaks of sunshine after rain. It's time to turn your dreams into reality. The future is looking rosy. You lay the groundwork to develop goals sustainably. You benefit from a stable environment that offers a wellspring of potential. You invest energy in a functional and practical area. It brings a time of nurturing your home environment and using latent talents. Life improves through your willingness to work on the nuts and bolts of daily goals. As the pace slows down, you can savor a journey that restores harmony and equilibrium.

It gets you on course to develop your talents and expand your skillset. It amplifies your abilities and nurtures creativity. You have qualities that seek expression. Nurturing your environment brings a path that is enriching and rewarding. It draws an active and dynamic chapter that sees you on track to progress forward. It improves foundations and provides an opportunity to develop a goal.

It brings a high note into your world. It sets the tone for developing your life towards a great destination. It captures the essence of excitement and brings success to the forefront of your life. It is a creative and potent time that draws blessings. Changes are on the horizon, a new adventure comes calling. You accomplish a great deal by exploring new options. It leads to growth and creates space for a meaningful journey.

New Moon in Leo and the Delta Aquarids Meteor Shower bring unscripted adventures that deliver fun and excitement. It brings a soul-stirring time of discovery. You are on a mission to improve your circumstances; impending communication brings a boost to your spirit. Life reveals a curious twist when someone intriguing reaches out soon.

You can move forward and adjust to the changes that swirl around your environment while nurturing your spirit. More structure and stability emerge from being mindful of the path ahead. It brings a busy time, and delegating tasks could be a useful tool to lighten the load. Something you've dearly been waiting for arrives with a flourish. It brings a positive aspect and is a cause for celebration. Your willingness to explore possibilities brings a winning chapter. It sets the tone for a cycle of growth as you generate a path that draws adventures and excitement. A cluster of social interactions and a buzz of fresh energy leave you feeling inspired.

A decision ahead brings a lighter chapter. It helps you make the best move forward. It encourages the type of expansion that supports well-being and self-development. An initiative comes calling, and it offers the chance to dive into a path of wisdom and inspiration. It helps reboot and rejuvenate your energy. It does launch a direction that is in alignment with the person you are becoming.

AUGUST

Sun	Mon	Tue	Wed	Thu	Fri	Sat
	1	2	3	4	5	6
7	8	9	10	11	12	13
14	15	16	17	18	19	20
21	22	23	24	25	26	27
28	29	30	31			

August 5th - First Quarter Moon Scorpio 11:06

August 8th - Full Moon in Aquarius Supermoon 01:35. Sturgeon Moon.

August 8th - Perseids Meteor Shower July 17th - August 24th

August 14th - Saturn at Opposition

August 19th - Last Quarter Moon in Taurus 04:36

August 27th - New Moon in Virgo 08:16

August 27th - Mercury at Greatest Eastern Elongation at 27.3 degrees from the Sun

NEW MOON

FULL MOON

A surge of optimism lets luck into your life. It sees you becoming involved with an area that offers room to progress. It creates a stable foundation that illuminates a lighter environment. Being open to change helps craft a vision that lets you journey towards achieving a long-held goal. It has you feeling more hopeful about prospects. It does nurture a supportive environment.

Lighter energy is coming that lifts your spirits. It brings a happy-go-lucky aspect that washes away troubles. An idea crystallizes into being and brings a path that draws excitement. It does have you on course to expand your world. It brings an innovative and creative chapter of immersing yourself in a passion project. A social aspect brings a lively and supportive environment. There is plenty to celebrate as you set off in a new direction. Releasing the shadows lets you focus on a meaningful area that draws abundance.

Surprise communication arrives from someone who has been out of the loop lately. It takes you to a new book of chapters. Indeed, it brings a beautiful time of sharing memories and going over gossip and news. It brings the encouraging potential to the forefront of your social life. A rise in memories and emotions gets a nurturing environment that opens a delightful box of exciting possibilities. It connects you with a happy and engaging chapter that brings a sense of rejuvenation and renewal.

Full Moon in Aquarius Supermoon and the Perseids Meteor Shower this week brings a lucky break. It reveals a connected environment that helps you unwind and relax with friends. There is plenty to feel happy about, as the area, you focus your energy on brings enrichment. It plots a course towards a path that you cherish and appreciate. There is compelling energy brewing in the background of your social life. Foundations become secure, and this stability offers a smoother trajectory forward. Little goes under your radar as you spot a diamond in the rough. It marks a time of expansion that provides growth.

Indeed, you reveal a brighter chapter; it brings a shift that draws harmony and wellness. It speaks about getting involved with a passion project. There is a focus on freedom and expansion that rejuvenates your spirit. It does bring the development of a bond, and you get a chance to flex your social muscle and get involved with catching up with friends and colleagues. It brings a lovely time that sparkles with good fortune, and it soon gives you insight into inspiring possibilities. Your imagination ignites with creative offerings; it brings a cornucopia of refreshing options from which to grow your world. There are lovely indications that fulfillment of a dream arrives, which releases the issues that have held you back. You reveal happy surprises and enjoy a sense of support that triggers growth and advancement.

You head to a chapter that holds great promise. It's one that closes the door on past issues, which lets you settle into a new groove of developing your skills. It lifts the lid on a chapter that enriches your life. Positive influences bring freedom and expansion. Banishing the barriers that limit progress lets new options flow into your world. Investing in your abilities draws dividends as a new role is on offer soon.

After a bumpy ride, you iron out the wrinkles and enjoy a time of stability. It does see things are progressing forwards. If you have been struggling with uncertainty, you soon resolve the confusion. It lets you take a leap of faith and embrace developing a curious journey. It brings a bountiful cycle that gently unfurls over time. Your flexibility and perseverance bring dividends.

You enter a richly abundant environment that offers scope to nurture a bond of the heart. It brings magic and mayhem as you embark on new adventures with someone special. Rising fortunes get a shot of good luck that tips the scales in your favor. This person is engaging, attentive, and a good communicator. You cook up a storm with a kindred spirit who is a lively companion. It brings a memorable time of sharing thoughts and ideas.

In Virgo this week, New Moon combined with Mercury at Greatest Eastern Elongation from the Sun to heighten potential. A build-up of pressure and responsibilities put your performance to the test. Prioritizing the essential areas helps streamline the process, and this lets you work effectively. There is a lot of activity coming into your career sector; some surprises along the way give you feedback. It lights a path towards prestigious success in the workplace. Your career path has several twists and turns along the way before receiving a boost.

Life brims with new potential. It's a swift-moving environment that draws new possibilities to light. An active and productive chapter attracts a positive influence that offers the key to growing your abilities. You receive an offer over the coming weeks. Take time to contemplate your future direction, and choose using the power of your intellect and intuition combined.

A useful avenue opens soon. It brings an influence that captures the essence of dreams and aspirations. Going after your vision brings an exciting chapter of discovery. You pour your energy into a unique project and delight in creating a master plan towards your goals. You are on a continuous cycle of growth and change; this elevates your abilities and advances your situation.

SEPTEMBER

Sun	Mon	Tue	Wed	Thu	Fri	Sat
				1	2	3
4	5	6	7	8	9	10
11	12	13	14	15	16	17
18	19	20	21	22	23	24
25	26	27	28	29	30	

September 7th - First Quarter Moon Sagittarius 18:08

September 10th - Mercury Retrograde begins in Libra

September 10th - Corn Moon. Harvest Moon. Full Moon in Pisces 09:58

September 16th - Neptune at Opposition

September 17th - Last Quarter Moon in Gemini 21:52

September 23 - Mabon/Fall Equinox. 01:03

September 25th - New Moon in Libra 21:54

September 26th - Jupiter at Opposition

FULL MOON

As you chart a course towards developing your life, you discover someone you can lean on for support and guidance. You find out opportunities that take your artistic talents to the next level. It is a highly creative time that sees you operating effectively and efficiently. Considering your options offers the chance to upgrade your circumstances. Life becomes more dynamic, active, and exciting.

There are power and strength in your spirit that gives you the determination to push back barriers and expand horizons. As you take a bold step forward, you discover a pathway that creates a change of direction. It may involve a new approach to life in general. News, messages, and answers come swiftly during this productive and active time. It clears the decks and creates space for a new flow of possibilities to tempt you forward.

You get news about a deal soon. It begins a voyage that offers room to progress your life. It is a time of rediscovering ambition and plotting the course towards your vision. You get a broader sense of what is possible when you set your sights on a lofty goal. An offer ahead gets the ball rolling on an enterprising chapter that advances a journey forward. Growth and prosperity light the way ahead.

Mercury Retrograde begins in Libra. Harvest Moon. Full Moon in Pisces When life throws a curveball, it's wise to explore new options. It is a time that helps you break fresh ground with news and information likely to be incoming in rapid-fire. Advancement comes knocking and lets you open the door to a new chapter of growing your abilities and using your talents to steller effect. Having options at your disposal opens the door to a busy time that nourishes stability.

You can ride out any turbulence and set sail towards smoother waters. The more you learn, the more you distill it down into your unique brand of wisdom and knowledge. Focusing on implementing practical strategies de-clutters thought processes and helps prioritize the right path forward. It provides stable foundations that draw balance even during uncertain times such as this. As old challenges begin to melt away, it opens the door to a chapter of growing your life and expanding your reach into new areas. Using an experimental flavor to life helps you harness the essence of creativity and explore pathways towards growth.

You can adjust course as necessary and ride out the turbulence of Mercury retrograde. Evaluating the direction ahead brings a new and exciting landscape into focus. It lets you make your mark on developing an area that offers growth and prosperity. It orients you towards using your skills and refining your talents. Indeed, a trailblazing approach supports a rewarding outcome.

This week is more important than you may realize. It starts a new cycle that adds weight to your professional goals. It brings a productive time that sees you working hard to progress your vision forward. You begin to see signs that things are shaping up the right way to improve your bottom line. It brings a bonus that draws stability. It is a time of progress that offers a new source of possibility to explore.

Creativity is heightening, which links you to nurturing your artistic talents. It helps reinvent potential, and this sees you draw balance and stability into your world. An area you become involved with becomes one of your most fantastic leads. It opens a chapter that brings good cheer and joy. It helps you reap the benefits of a more connected and social environment. It offers a highly productive time that lets you bid farewell to setbacks. It becomes a journey of enormous personal growth. It leads to a busy time of gaining mastery over a new skill.

Information arrives that triggers activity around your social life. It lets you welcome in a new start and an emphasis on nurturing bonds. As life expands, you share thoughts and ideas with the person who offers remarkable insight into the path ahead. It does smooth any frazzled edges and brings you to a curious chapter that enriches. Screening out distractions lets you focus on the area that holds meaning. It gives your life depth, purpose, structure, and balance. It opens the door to a brighter environment that warms your world.

Mabon/Fall Equinox. New Moon in Libra. Jupiter at Opposition. Embracing the emotional sanctuary you have created for your energy does have you wanting to take things slowly. You may feel reflective and introspective as memories ebb and flow. Taking time to release old emotions creates space for new possibilities to emerge. A chapter of social engagement and festivities loom overhead. Placing the bar higher draws dividends. It gives you time to catch your breath and explore possibilities gently. Changes ahead hit the right note in your life. It opens the portal towards progressing an area of interest. Life sparkles with new options as you make tracks towards improving your social life. The outcome is something that blesses your life on several levels. You touch down on a chapter that offers warmth and companionship, and this brings a boost.

You face a crossroads, which relates to growth in your career path. There may be some learning on offer that takes your vision further than you currently realize possible. An expansive vista tempts you towards change. Unhook from areas that distract or encourage procrastination. A focused effort allows you to hone in on your most important life goals. Focusing on the priorities draws a path littered with golden options. It delivers a wake-up call that encourages you to move out of your comfort zone. It brings fresh energy that reboots the potential possible.

OCTOBER

Sun	Mon	Tue	Wed	Thu	Fri	Sat
						1
2	3	4	5	6	7	8
9	10	11	12	13	14	15
16	17	18	19	20	21	22
23	24	25	26	27	28	29
30	31					

October 2nd - Mercury Retrograde ends in Virgo

October 3rd - First Quarter Moon in Capricorn 00.14

October 7th - Draconids Meteor Shower. Oct 6th -10th

October 8th - Mercury Greatest Western Elongation

October 9th - Hunters Moon. Full Moon in Aries 20:54

October 17th - Last Quarter Moon in Cancer 17.15

October 21st -Orionids Meteor Shower. October 2nd - November 7th

October 25th - New Moon in Scorpio 10:48

October 25th - Partial Solar Eclipse

Mercury Retrograde ends in Virgo this week. It sparks evolution for your social life. It brings communication that blossoms into nurturing a bond. As your emotional foundations stabilize, you get involved with the soul project that inspires your heart. It does have you connecting with someone who has thoughtful ideas and a tender approach. This person is quiet yet intriguing as they offer a soul-stirring perspective on life.

Touching down in a social environment adds the touch of magic and mayhem to your life. It brings an energizing time that hits a high note as you explore the synergy with someone who inspires your awareness. It brings an open road of adventure that is a saving grace as it gives you a suitable outlet for your restless energy. This person coaxes you out of your comfort zone; they spark lively discussions that are sure to be memorable. A sense of kinship and companionship nurture the foundations of your home life. It brings a happy time that captures your imagination

Having more choices for your social life aligns you towards a chapter of personal growth. It lets you chart a lively course towards expansion. It brings a supportive aspect that nurtures well-being. Your emotional awareness feels drawn to open expression with this person. It marks a significant chapter that becomes a gateway from which to grow your world.

A Full Moon in Aries illuminates rejuvenation. It lets you release your worries and begin to heal. After a time of soul-searching, you touch down on a path that highlights new options. Placing one foot in front of the other lets you move forward with purpose. The harsh lessons of the past fade away, creating space for a bold journey ahead.

You are ready for the transformation ahead. It gives you the ability to wipe the slate clean and start a new chapter. It is a line in the sand that represents healing. Once you cross over, you enter a portal that triggers new possibilities. It brings moments to treasure. Your life fills with magic and excitement. Your social life expands and takes you towards an original environment that brings people into your world. It unleashes creativity and brings you opportunities to collaborate and work together on a joint project.

Your social life benefits from lightness and harmony when a valued companion bridges the gap. This person has been out of the loop and reaches out with a thoughtful note of communication. It brings the chance to share thoughts and ideas with someone smart and insightful. You are compatible with this individual and soon make plans to catch up more often. Hearing from this person leaves you feeling energized and ready to tackle a new journey forward. It plants the seeds that grow over the coming months. You may feel jittery or nervous at first, but their warmth disarms and enriches.

It is a time that grows your world. You cut away from areas that are no longer relevant. It removes the drama and stress. Communication arrives to tempt you out into the community. It brings fresh energy to your social life. It does kick off a journey that draws improvement into your life. You are on the cusp of change, and this draws opportunities and adventure into your world. It does plant the seeds for a new chapter. A compelling way opens, and you thrive in a social environment.

Something on offer hits the sweet spot for your life. It triggers an active phase of growth. The movement and discovery ahead speak of the change that is possible when you expand your horizons. You make progress on developing an endeavor that offers room to secure advancement. Seeing more stability in your life lets you thrive in a more grounded environment. You are ready to sweep away all that stands in the way of you and your vision.

A unique option is coming that gives you a chance to grow the dream. It sees things becoming busy when events turn in your favor. It lets you hone in on an exciting new endeavor. As you lift the lid on a fresh chapter of potential, your inspiration burns brightly. Something on offer captures your interest and allows you to take your talents to the next level. It shines a light on lively discussions and group activities that blend well with your goals.

New Moon in Scorpio with a Partial Solar Eclipse delivers a focus on self-development that gets you involved in exploring pathways of learning and growth. It brings the landscape of possibility and inspiration. Motivation is running high. Your life expands all it touches. It is a time that improves your life's basic structure, and this secures a strong foundation from which to grow your goals. You achieve a great deal by exploring your options and plotting a course forward.

It clears the decks for the new potential to emerge. It brings a busy time where you will have a lot going on. You can take a proactive approach and develop your dreams. Adopting a broad perspective brings new possibilities that inspire you creatively. It is an essential journey of self-discovery that empowers your spirit and enriches your life.

A cycle of good fortune that kicks off a chapter of progressing your dreams. It does highlight information and wisdom gained in the past can now assist you in moving forward. You break the chain of restriction that has kept you locked in a limiting pattern. New potential arrives, and this brings the news and information. It sparks a transition towards developing a journey that inspires your heart and soul. Before long, you enter a cycle that sees you accomplish a great deal. You may have many balls in the air during this time, but you soon learn to juggle them adeptly.

NOVEMBER

Sun	Mon	Tue	Wed	Thu	Fri	Sat
		1	2	3	4	5
6	7	8	9	10	11	12
13	14	15	16	17	18	19
20	21	22	23	24	25	26
27	28	29	30			

November 1st - First Quarter Moon in Aquarius 06.37

November 4th - Taurids Meteor Shower. September 7th - December 10th

November 8th - Full Moon in Taurus 11:01 Beaver Moon. November 8th - Total Lunar Eclipse

November 9th - Uranus at Opposition

November 16th - Last Quarter Moon in Leo 13:27

November 17th - Leonids Meteor Shower Nov 6th-30th

November 23rd - New Moon in Sagittarius 22:57

November 30th - First Quarter Moon Pisces 14:36

FULL MOON

Taurids Meteor Shower releases uncertainty or confusion when new information arrives that lights the path forward. It brings expansive boundaries that lighten the load and delivers an influx of happiness. It brings a social chapter that draws new friendships, and it also connects you with treasured companions. You reawaken to the rich landscape of potential that surrounds your world.

It brings a growth-driven chapter that opens new pathways. It sets in motion the ideal conditions to shift your focus forward. As you launch your ship of dreams, you begin a dynamic chapter of developing your vision. Information arrives that sets the tone for a productive time of change. It brings foundations that improve your home life, which helps guide your objectives as it creates a stable basis from which to grow your goals.

It lets you engage with a broader world of possibilities. It brings a transition, and this starts a new journey that connects you with others who hold similar goals. It brings a foundation that provides you with a stable basis from which to grow your social life. Pleasant surprises flow into your world as you begin to see life from a different perspective.

A serendipitous pathway connects you with a personal vision. Change is arriving, and these dreams help you take note of signs that pinpoint the correct direction forward. Setting intentions and maintaining a positive approach bring new possibilities.

Full Moon in Taurus combines with a Total Lunar Eclipse this week. Releasing guilt brings healing. It helps release unexpected emotions and lets you step up and own the lessons learned. Sweeping away outworn energy creates space to focus on your dreams. It does connect you with others who come in to assist your journey forward. It kicks off new possibilities that inspire growth. An attractive viewpoint broadens the scope of potential. It touches you down in a landscape that offers a breakthrough. Endless possibilities fascinate as you push back barriers and enjoy new adventures. It opens the doors to a journey that brings happiness and harmony into focus.

As issues are released, your attention draws an area that offers progression. It solves the riddle for your restless energy and brings a busy time that fills your life with new possibilities. Life holds a curious twist as a unique option emerges that tempts you towards expansion. It is the giver of renewal and happiness. It lights up pathways that improve social bonds and friendships.

You forge a connection with a supportive person who eases life's challenges. This person is capable of coming up with new solutions and ideas that inspire growth. They have inside advice and guidance that support a journey that elevates your situation. It does mark a time of significant improvement to your social life.

Leonids Meteor Shower brings a landmark moment; it is a gateway toward a brighter future. There are lots of changes on the way for your social life. It leaves you feeling valued. As communication tumbles into your life, you see an interwoven awareness of the connection that forms a structure of support in your life. It magnifies potential and transitions you towards developing a bond that captures your interest. It does have you feeling spontaneous and acting on impulse with this person. It shines a light on wellness and harmony. It lets you walk over a bridge to a new landscape of refreshing possibility. You build foundations that offer stability and structure. It marks a time that rules social expansion.

Life sprinkles the fairy dust of new possibilities. It lets you treat yourself to nurturing bonds. A positive influence entices personal growth. It links you up with the person who offers ideas, stimulating conversations, and support. It helps you rebound from hurdles and deflect negativity. It brings substance to your spirit that draws stability.

It does bring light energy that is beautiful and poetic. Life comes full circle and gets an opportunity to nurture a bond. It is the continuation of a more comprehensive theme of change that currently surrounds your social life. It brings an enriching phase that draws harmony and abundance.

New Moon in Sagittarius delivers an energizing time that hits a high note. It gives you the green light to embrace a more social environment. It has elements that offer harmony, advice, guidance, and wisdom. It takes you towards a lively and active chapter that enriches your social life. As you unwrap the path ahead, you explore nurturing a situation that soothes your restless spirit. It flings open the door to a chapter that brings change on a personal level. You are ready to unpack a new chapter, and the experience ahead supports your vision. As you explore a diverse range of pathways, you move in a direction that draws new options into your world. There is a change that creates a shift towards your vision. Your inner guidance system is the compass that guides you correctly forward. Complications soon fade away, the sunshine blooms in your life. News arrives that draws excitement and adventure.

There are opportunities ahead that improve the security available in your world. You benefit from new ideas and options that flow into your life. It makes for a refreshing chapter that inspires your mind, and this is the catalyst for growth. An original and innovative path forward is a route that speaks to your creativity. It rules a way of expansion that brings a new area of learning. It multiplies the goodness in your life; it elevates your talents and gets the ball rolling on advancing your vision for the future.

DECEMBER

Sun	Mon	Tue	Wed	Thu	Fri	Sat
				1	2	3
4	5	6	7	8	9	10
11	12	13	14	15	16	17
18	19	20	21	22	23	24
25	26	27	28	29	30	31

December 8th - Cold Moon. Moon Before Yule
December 8th - Full Moon in Gemini 04:07
December 8th - Mars at Opposition

December 13th - Geminids Meteor Shower. Dec 7th- 17th

December 16th - Last Quarter Moon in Virgo 08:56

December 21st - Ursids Meteor Shower December 17 - 25th December 21 - Mercury at Greatest Eastern elongation.
December 21st - Yule/Winter Solstice at 09:48

December 23rd - New Moon in Capricorn 10:16

December 29th - Mercury Retrograde begins in Capricorn

December 30th - First Quarter Moon Aries 01:21

FULL MOON

You've been through an unpredictable time recently, but there is exciting potential brewing in your life's background. It makes itself known soon and clears the slate for a fresh chapter. Information arrives that shakes up the potential. It invigorates your spirit and offers an opportunity for growth. Incorporating this news into your plans is a pivotal moment. It unleashes your talents in an area ripe for progression. Exploring leads soon lets you head towards a direction that draws stable foundations. It allows you to reach for something more, and you soon enter an extended time of developing goals.

News arrives that helps you stay on top of the game in your working life. Many changes are surrounding your industry, and exploring new technologies, places you in the right alignment to capitalize on your talents. You benefit from a flexible and pragmatic approach as you prepare to embark on a new journey forward. Carefully exploring options lets you obtain due diligence before embarking on your next chapter of growth.

A dear friend returns in your life, and this kicks off a chapter of sharing treasured memories. It does bring changes that stabilize foundations. It sees you improving your living situation. This person is smart and insightful; they open doors and bring generosity and wisdom to the table. It draws advancement into your home life and triggers an active phase of developing a bond that sparks potential.

Full Moon in Gemini and Mars at Opposition gives the go-ahead to develop your life and move into an area that seems tailor-made for your vision. It brings an environment that stimulates your imagination and ideas. Creative expression, mingling with kindred spirits, discovering the right outlet for your talents brings a trend that liberates stress. Indeed, it is constructive for you to work on personal goals. It brings many reasons to be happy.

Exciting opportunities are coming into your world that dazzle and delight. Helpful communication jumpstarts a friendship. It's a chance to share dialogue and improve a bond. You enter a productive chapter that keeps you on your toes with new possibilities. It ramps up the activity in your social life. It places you in strong shape to improve your circumstances and chart a compelling course forward.

You discover a situation that has you feeling a warm glow. It brings a positive influence that sets the scene to nurture abundance. Connecting with this individual is helpful to you; it activates a time of sharing thoughts and ideas. It gives you a chance to improve your social life and nurture your well-being. Technology plays an integral part in keeping the situation connected. It sees life becoming productive and enjoyable. Life becomes a significant hub of activity that is rewarding. Your emotional life and the warmth of friendship and fun bring happiness into view.

Ursids Meteor Shower. Mercury at Greatest Eastern elongation. Yule/Winter Solstice at week's end. This cosmic alignment shows that something substantial is occurring in your life. It launches a new chapter towards an area that holds promise. Heightened social opportunities have you enjoying enlivening conversations with friends and companions. You make a new acquaintance, and this person adds the sparkle and shine to your social life. A lucky break takes you towards an enriching environment that is ripe with celebration.

Life gets an upgrade when someone in your neighborhood or extended social circle reaches out. It does see a path open towards a more connected bond as life begins to pick up steam. A stable landscape nourishes your life. Being open draws a new companion. Embracing life-affirming endeavors such as developing this bond attracts wellness and abundance. You blaze through an exciting time that sees you making progress on a personal dream. It does bring rapid changes, creating space to release all that stands in the way between you and happiness. It is a time that brings magic. It's a theme of improving circumstances that draw enriching moments. There is a surprise nestled in the chapter ahead, which leads to a celebration. Limitations break down, and opportunity comes knocking; you enter a transformational chapter that draws harmony and abundance. A social environment brings a sense of connection and community into focus.

New Moon in Capricorn. Mercury Retrograde begins this week. There is a change ahead that awakens you to an environment of self-development and personal growth. It is a time that offers blessings as new potential sweeps in, and this revolutionizes your vision. Life changes at the drop of the dime; it brings you in contact with someone who plays an integral part in future events. You move forward towards a fresh start. Chasing your dreams is the first step towards embracing a journey of the heart.

You are approaching a path that brings an exciting possibility. It tempts you towards change, and it's an environment that offers room to grow your life. It does have you feeling energized and willing to tackle new projects. It gives you an expansive view of what is possible in your world when you set your mind to developing new possibilities. It helps you tap into your boundless creativity and come up with a winning endeavor. It draws a time of increasing stability that brings a secure and grounded foundation.

Exciting new possibilities are arriving soon. It links you up to a chapter that allows you to find hidden gems of potential. It brings a clear direction that opens a path forward. It brings a different type of journey that orientates you towards a time of discovery and adventure. You pursue an enticing interest with an openness that is refreshing. You usher in change and can create growth by expanding your horizons into new areas. It helps you forge a path that is unique and allows your talents to flourish under sunny skies.

Dear Stargazer,

I hope you have enjoyed planning your year with the stars utilizing Astrology and Zodiac influences. My yearly zodiac books feature a weekly (four weeks to a month) horoscope. You can find me on the sites below, where you can get personal astrology or intuitive readings.

https://www.facebook.com/SiaSands

Instagram: SiaSands

You can order an Astrology reading at:

https://psychic-emails.com/

Leaving a review is welcomed and appreciated.

Many Blessings,

Sia Sands